SWINDON TO GLOUCESTER

INCLUDING THE CIRENCESTER AND TETBURY BRANCHES

Vic Mitchell and Keith Smith

MP Middleton Press

Cover picture: Kemble was busy on 10th May 1963 as 2-6-2T no. 6137 returned to Brimscombe after having assisted a Gloucester to Paddington train over the summit. No. D7020 waits to follow it, while an AC railbus stands in the bay for Cirencester trains. (Nelson coll./T.Walsh)

Published January 2005

ISBN 1 904474 46 2

© Middleton Press, 2005

Design David Pede

Published by
> *Middleton Press*
> *Easebourne Lane*
> *Midhurst, West Sussex*
> *GU29 9AZ*

Tel: 01730 813169
Fax: 01730 812601
Email: info@middletonpress.co.uk
www.middletonpress.co.uk

Printed & bound by Biddles Ltd, Kings Lynn

INDEX

ACKNOWLEDGEMENTS

We are very grateful for the assistance received from many of those mentioned in the credits also to A.E.Bennett, L.Crosier, G.Croughton, D.Edge, D.Hyde, N.Langridge, M.Oakley, D.T.Rowe, Mr D. and Dr S.Salter, R.E.Toop, and our ever supportive wives, Barbara Mitchell and Janet Smith.

I.   Railway Clearing House map for 1947. The grey lines are GWR and the black ones are LMSR. It excludes most of the halts.

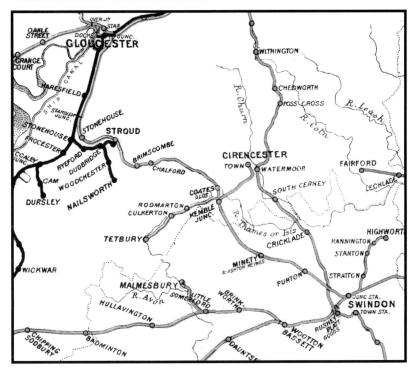

GEOGRAPHICAL SETTING

Swindon developed in the railway age and is situated at the foot of the Chalk mass of the Marlborough Downs. The route runs across fairly level Wealden Clays and Sands in the vicinity of the headwaters of the River Thames until running onto the dip slope of the Cotswold Hills at Kemble.

The summit of this Limestone ridge is penetrated in Sapperton Tunnel, the two branches being largely constructed on this material. The descent is through the Golden Valley, which is incised deeply in this yellow/golden rock.

The steep inclination of the River Frome in this area allowed the development of many mills which have spawned a variety of industries. These produced traffic for the Thames & Severn Canal and later the railway.

At Stonehouse, the line emerges from the narrow Golden Valley and runs north on the wide expanses of Lias Clay and Alluvium that flank the River Severn south of the ancient cathedral city of Gloucester.

The boundary between Wiltshire and Gloucestershire is between Minety and Kemble. It ran across the entrance to Tetbury station in its early years.

The maps are to the scale of 25ins to 1 mile, with north at the top, unless otherwise indicated.

HISTORICAL BACKGROUND

Great Western Railway trains from London were passing the site of Swindon station to a temporary terminus three miles to the west of it at Hay Lane from 17th December 1840. They continued on to Bristol from 30th June 1841. However, a station was not provided at Swindon until July 1842.

The Birmingham & Gloucester Railway came into use in 1840. Another early line in the area was that of the Bristol & Gloucester Railway which opened in 1844 and they both became part of the Midland Railway in 1845. The South Wales Railway opened in 1850 between Chepstow and Swansea. It reached Gloucester in 1851, becoming part of the GWR in 1862.

The Cheltenham & Great Western Union Railway Act was passed on 21st June 1836 and the line was opened from Swindon to Cirencester on 31st May 1841. There was no station at Kemble until 12th May 1845, when trains began running through to Gloucester. The C&GWUR lines were leased to the GWR to operate and were laid to the broad gauge of 7ft 0¼ins. They were engineered by I.K.Brunel, the through route having double track. The C&GWUR was purchased by the GWR on 1st July 1843.

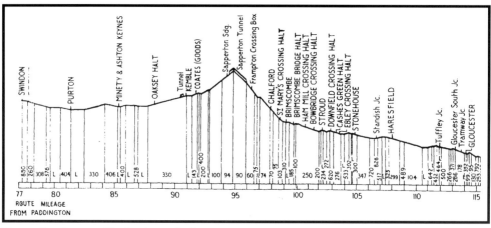

II.	Gradient profile for the main line.

The Gloucester-Bristol section was also broad gauge, but it was converted to standard gauge on 22nd May 1854. This meant that the GWR had to provide separate tracks for the eight miles south of Gloucester until its own lines in the area were similarly converted on 26th May 1872.

The route and the rest of the GWR came into the Western Region of British Railways upon nationalisation in 1948. Privatisation preparations in March 1994 resulted in InterCity operating between London and Cheltenham. Regional Railways provided local services. The former became part of the franchise of Great Western Trains on 4th February 1996 and the latter was operated by Prism Rail's Wales & West from October 13th of that year. This company became Wessex Trains in 2001, but from May of that year until September 2002 alternate local trains were operated by GWT and Virgin CrossCountry. The changes have been more frequent subsequently and have involved WT again!

Cirencester Branch

The service began on 31st May 1841 with through trains from London. It was largely operated as a branch from July 1844.

Little changed until 6th April 1964 when the line closed to passengers, goods traffic ceasing on 4th October 1965.

Tetbury Branch

The route opened on 2nd December 1889, closing to freight on 5th August 1963 and to passengers on 6th April 1964.

It was originally intended that the town should be served by an extension of the Nailsworth branch, but the work was abandoned east of that place in the 1860s.

PASSENGER SERVICES

Down trains running at least five days per week on the full length of the route are considered in this section.

Main Line

The initial timetable offered seven trains on weekdays through to Cirencester; there were six upon opening to Gloucester. For most of the nineteenth century there were nine on weekdays and two on Sundays.

Below are some sample frequencies:

	Weekdays	Sundays
1901	11	3
1910	13	3
1930	8	5
1950	9	5

An all stations and halts service between Chalford and Stonehouse began on 12th October 1903. The steam railmotor ran hourly and was extended to Gloucester in 1921. It ran half-hourly from 1922 and two trips were soon extended to Kemble. The service was greatly reduced by 1950 and ceased on 2nd November 1964.

For many years there was one train shown from Swindon to Kemble only. It was often an operational convenience, which allowed a branch train to be serviced. The stopping pattern varied greatly, some expresses calling only at Kemble and Stroud, but not Swindon.

In 1970 there were ten weekday and six Sunday trains and by 1983 the figures were 16 and 7. Most started from Swindon, with only a couple of peak-hour London trains. Thirty years later the figures were similar, but with more trains running east of Swindon.

Cirencester Branch

First we will consider weekday services. The initial seven trains soon dropped to six, but by 1872 the figure was nine. Seven or eight were run in the 1890s, but from 1902 it was 14, a similar frequency being maintained into World War I. It was cut to ten in 1916, eight in 1917 and from April 1918, it was only six as the country struggled to survive.

By 1921 nine trains were run, the figure being eleven in most years up to World War II. In September 1939, it was cut to three, but restored to eight during 1940 as there was a heavy military traffic developing.

Nine or ten trains were the norm from 1946 until the introduction of railbuses in 1959, when 13 or 14 trips were operated, with 17 on Saturdays.

Sunday services comprised two journeys from about 1850 to 1915 and records show that this frequency was resumed in 1940. It was increased to four trips from 1947 to the end.

KEMBLE and CIRENCESTER.

Miles	Down.		Week Days.	Sundays.	Up.		Week Days.	Sundays.
			mrn mrn mrn a aft aft aft aft aft S aft	....			nun mn mrn aft aft aft aft aft S	....
	Kemble [76, 77	dp	8 40 9 50 10 28 11 40 12 47 1 22 2 25 3 5 4 0 5 25 6 47 8 4 8 39	....	Cirencester D	dp	8 0 9 23 10 5 11 10 12 27 2 43 3 30 4 50 6 15 7 40 8 18	....
4¼	Cirencester D	ar	8 50 9 58 10 38 11 48 12 55 1 32 2 33 3 13 4 10 5 33 6 55 8 12 8 47	....	Kemble 72, 73	ar	8 9 9 31 10 13 11 18 12 35 2 50 3 45 5 2 6 25 7 50 8 26	....

a Mondays only.　　　D Town ; over ½ mile to Watermoor Station.　　　S Saturdays only.

Nov - 1930

Tetbury Branch

Early timetables showed five weekday trains, but this was increased to six in 1898, a figure that was maintained in most years until February 1959, when railbuses offered eight return trips.

There was one Sunday train from about 1910 to 1939, but it was intended mainly for milk conveyance. One weekday train was withdrawn during World War II, but only for a short period.

KEMBLE and TETBURY.—Great Western.

	gov mrn non aft gov	Up.	gov aft aft aft gov	
Paddington Station, LONDON 4 . . . . dep	5 30 10 20 12 0 3 0 5 45	Tetbury . . . . dep	7 55 12 15 2 20 3 50 7 5	arrives 6 00 at 3rd class
Kemble . . . . dep	8 35 1 5 5 0 5 25 8 0	Culkerton	8 5 12 35 2 30 4 0 7 15	
Culkerton	8 46 1 16 3 11 5 36 8 11	Kemble 34 to 36 arr	8 15 12 34 2 39 4 9 7 25	
Tetbury . . . . arr	8 55 1 24 3 19 5 44 8 19	LONDON (Pad.) 8 4 10 45 2 48 5 15 6 30 10 20		

Feb - 1890

KEMBLE and TETBURY.—Great Western.

Miles	Down.		Week Days.	Suns.		Up.		Week Days.	Suns.
			mrn mrn aft aft aft aft aft	aft	Miles			mrn mrn mrn aft aft aft	aft
	Kemble . . . . . . dep	8 40 10 0 1 8 3 42 5 20 8 17	7 10		Tetbury . . . . dep	7 55 9 15 11 55 2 46 4 5 7	5 6 13	
3	Rodmarton Platform	8 48 10 9 1 13 3 48 5 28 8 23	7 15	2¼	Culkerton	8 2 9 22 12 5 2 53 4 12 7 13	6 20	
4½	Culkerton	8 56 10 15 1 19 3 52 5 33 8 28	7 21	4½	Rodmarton Platform	8 5 9 25 12 8 2 55 4 15 7 17	6 22	
7¼	Tetbury . . . . arr	9 5 10 27 1 28 4 0 5 42 8 37	7 30	7¼	Kemble 58, 62 . . . arr	8 12 9 33 12 20 3 3 4 24 7 27	6 30	

July - 1910

KEMBLE and TETBURY.

Miles	Down.		Week Days.	Suns.		Up.		Week Days.	Suns.	NOTES.
			mrn mrn aft h aft aft aft aft		Miles			mrn mrn aft h aft aft aft	aft	h Runs on Tetbury
	Kemble . . . . . . dep	8 40 10 40 1 23 4 0 5 23 4 78 35 8 15			Tetbury . . . . dep	7 43 9 12 12 10 3 10 4 40 6 5 7 30 5 27		Monthly Market Day,
3	Rodmarton Platform	10 48 1 30 4 7 5 30 6 5 48 42 8 22		2¼	Culkerton	7 50 9 23 12 19 3 19 4 49 6 17 7 37 5 39		second Wednesday in
4½	Culkerton . . . . . . dep	8 50 10 57 1 35 4 12 5 35 6 79 8 47 8 27		4½	Rodmarton Platform	7 53 9 26 12 25 3 25 4 55 6 20 7 40 5 42		the month.
7¼	Tetbury . . . . . . arr	8 57 11 4 1 40 4 19 5 42 7 6 8 54 8 34		7¼	Kemble 72, 73 . . arr	8 0 9 33 12 32 3 32 5 7 6 27 7 47 5 49		

Nov - 1930

KEMBLE and TETBURY.

Miles	Down.		Week Days.	Sn		Up.		Week Days.	Sn	NOTES.
			U mrn mrn S aft h O aft aft	aft	Miles			mrn mrn SU E S h S E U aft aft S	aft	h Runs on Tetbury
	Kemble . . . . . . dep	7 15 8 40 10 30 12 15 1 20 4 0 5 35 6 50 8 37 9 35	8 7		Tetbury . . . . dep	7 50 9 15 11 45 12 15 12 45 3 10 4 40 5 0 6 5 7 35 9 8	5 30	Monthly Market Day
3	Rodmarton Platform	7 15 8 48 10 39 12 22 1 27 4 7 5 42 6 57 8 44 9 41	8 14	2¼	Culkerton	7 59 9 23 11 54 12 24 12 53 3 19 4 49 6 14 7 42 9 15	5 37	second Wednesday in
4½	Culkerton . . . . . . dep	7 19 8 52 10 47 12 26 1 31 4 12 5 46 7 1 8 48 9 45	8 18	4½	Rodmarton Platform	8 2 9 26 11 58 12 30 12 56 3 25 4 59 5 13 6 20 7 45 9 18	5 40	the month.
7¼	Tetbury . . . . . . arr	7 25 8 58 10 54 12 32 1 39 4 19 5 52 7 7 8 55 9 53	8 26	7¼	Kemble 74, 75 . . arr	8 9 9 33 12 9 12 38 1 3 3 33 5 7 5 24 6 28 7 52 9 25	5 47	O 12 mins earlier Sats

Aug - 1939

CHELTENHAM SPA EXPRESS

RESTAURANT CAR SERVICE

LONDON, KEMBLE, STROUD, GLOUCESTER and CHELTENHAM

WEEK DAYS

	pm			am
LONDON (Paddington) ...dep	4A55	Cheltenham Spa (St. James') ...dep		8A 0
		Cheltenham Spa (Malvern Rd.) „		8A 2
Kemble ... ...arr	6 33	Gloucester Central ... ... „		8A19
Stroud ... ... „	6 54	Stonehouse (Burdett Road)... „		8A33
Gloucester Central ... ... „	7 12	Stroud ... ... „		8A40
Cheltenham Spa (Malvern Rd.) „	7 33	Kemble ... ... „		9A 4
Cheltenham Spa (St. James') ... „	7 35	LONDON (Paddington) ...arr		10 35

A—Seats can be reserved in advance on payment of a fee of 2s. 0d. per seat

June - 1959

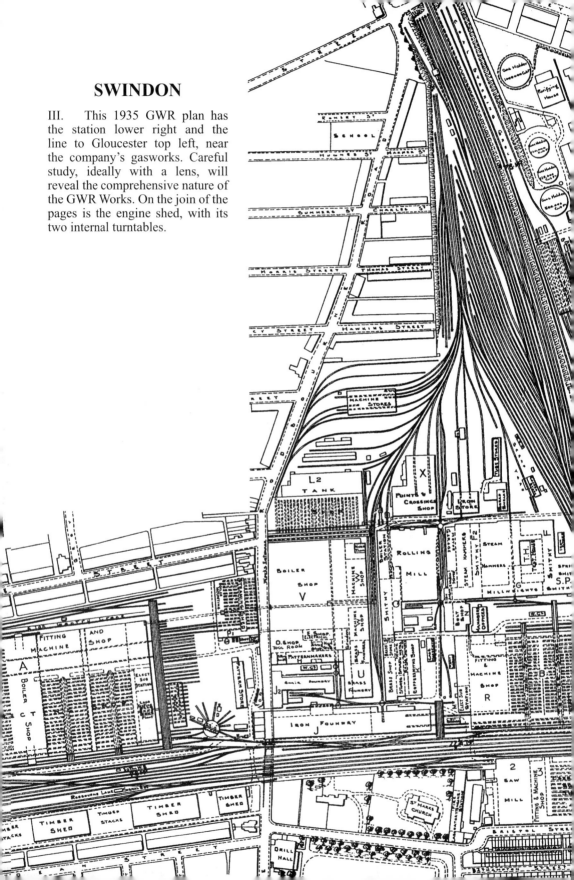

SWINDON

III. This 1935 GWR plan has the station lower right and the line to Gloucester top left, near the company's gasworks. Careful study, ideally with a lens, will reveal the comprehensive nature of the GWR Works. On the join of the pages is the engine shed, with its two internal turntables.

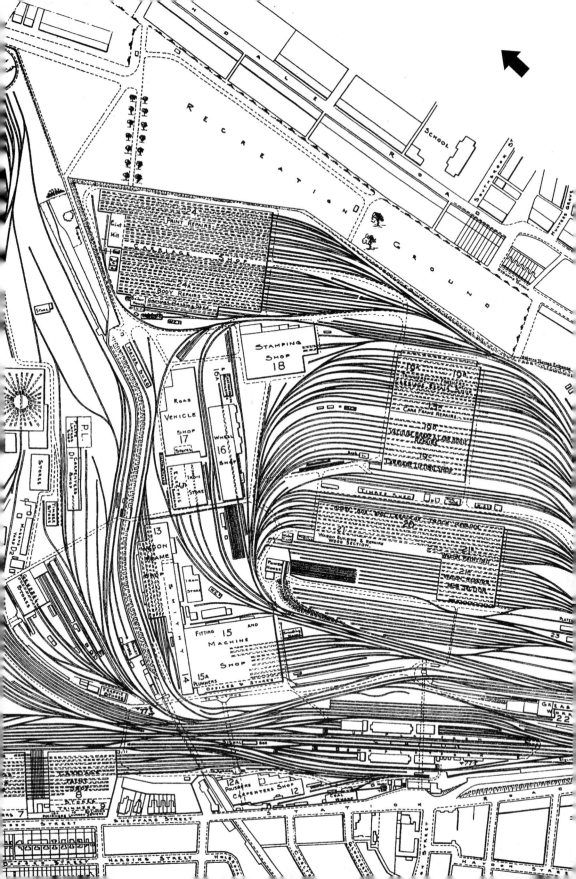

1.	The station opened on 17th July 1842, more than 12 months after the London to Cirencester service had begun. The first part of the 1843 Swindon Works is centre background and the left part of it is the engine shed. The line to Bristol is to the left of it and the Gloucester route curves to the right. (C.G.Maggs coll.)

2.	The down main platform (no. 4) is on the left. The footbridge lasted until October 1962; the 1870 subway is still in use. The up building was erected at the expense of a catering contractor for the benefit of whom all trains would stop for ten minutes. This contract was eventually terminated at vast cost in 1895. (Lens of Sutton)

3.   The presence of Swindon Works resulted in the population of the town increasing by a factor of 13 in 40 years. West Box had 174 levers and is opposite the junction of the Gloucester lines in this 1958 view from platform 5. (D.B.Clayton)

4.   With steam to spare and drain cocks open, no. 7035 Ogmore Castle accelerates a train for Gloucester past the works on 22nd April 1961. The pair of tracks parallel to the up line lead to the engine shed. Poor visibility formed a large part of an engineman's life. (M.A.N.Johnston)

5.	Platform 1 (right) had a through line, whilst nos 2 and 3 were bays. Local trains for Gloucester often started from these platforms, but on 24th April 1961 no. 9740 (right) was destined for Chippenham, while no. 4651 was about to depart at 5.55pm for Cirencester Watermoor. It would reverse at Swindon Town. (M.A.N.Johnston)

6.	No. D7050 is approaching platform 8 with freight from Gloucester on 24th May 1966. On the left is a three-road carriage shed, which was near the end of its life. On the right are the two "Engine Lines". (J.Day)

7.   The eight platforms were reduced to three on 3rd March 1968, when multiple aspect signalling was introduced. Of the old ones, only nos 5 and 8 were retained and all local signal boxes were closed. Standing at no. 3 (formerly 5) on 9th September 1991 is no. 6024 *King Edward I* with a special train to Cheltenham, while "Sprinter" no. 155310 runs ahead of it from platform 2 and an HST leaves from no. 1. No. 2 was a bay built on the site of the shed seen on the left of picture no. 6. (M.J.Stretton)

8.   Swindon Works once employed over 12,000 people, but closure came on 27th March 1986. It is seen behind the 11.32 Swansea to Paddington HST on 19th October 1991. These units were used on the Gloucester lines (right) for peak hour London-Cheltenham services. The shed on the right was for diesel fuelling and minor repairs. (M.J.Stretton)

9.　　An eastward view in April 2002 includes the 12-storey office block, erected in 1970-71 on the site of the original down buildings. A new booking hall was created on its ground floor, this linking direct with the subway. The platform in the centre was added in 1976 for mail and parcel traffic, plus occasional football specials. It was extended westward and opened for use by 60 trains per day from 2nd June 2003. Behind the roof is the signalling centre, which controls the route to a location one mile beyond Kemble. (V.Mitchell)

10.　　Standing at platform 1 on 18th January 2002 was "Adelante" no. 180104 on its last week of driver training on the Gloucester route. Performance is high, but so is noise level, as each coach has a diesel-electric system under the floor. (M.J.Stretton)

IV.　　The 1885 survey has the 1882 engine shed right of centre and the 1874 gasworks at the top, together with part of the North Wilts Canal, which once brought locomotive and domestic coal to the town. The majority of the works at that time is featured in the lower section, along with the Bristol lines. The signal box (centre) was designated "G" until replaced by a new one to the south of it on 22nd January 1909. Known as "Swindon Loco Yard", it was replaced on 27th January 1924 by one with 30 levers which lasted until 1968, when the line was singled to Kemble, from a point just beyond the left border of this map. The gasworks closed in January 1959. There had been an up goods loop in its vicinity from 1942 until 1966. Two miles northwest, Bremell Sidings were laid to a petrol store in 1943. They were used by Esso after the war, until 1987. The associated 25-lever signal box was closed in 1968.

Gas Works

SWINDON ENGINE SHED

Gasometers

Brick Works

11. The first shed north of the station came into use in 1872 and was for standard gauge stock. Use of the broad gauge shed west of the station diminished until closure in 1892. The new shed had nine roads and later had a turntable inside. Another such shed (right) followed, as shown on the map. This view is from the 1930s and features the original facade. (LPC/NRM)

Other pictures of the station and the works can be found in *Didcot to Swindon*, *Swindon to Bristol* and *Swindon to Newport*.

12. The eastern part of the "roundhouse" was completed in 1908 and all the radiating roads were fitted with substantial smoke hoods. This record is from 17th May 1931. (H.C.Casserley)

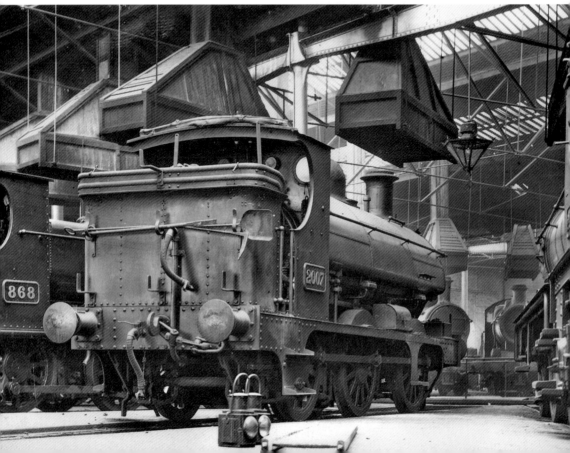

13.   To service the large allocation of locomotives, a massive coaling plant was erected, but shovels were used to load the hand-propelled tubs. One of these is about to be tipped into the tender of "Saint" class no. 2947 *Madresfield Court* on 4th July 1947. BR coded 82C, the shed closed on 2nd November 1964. (H.C.Casserley)

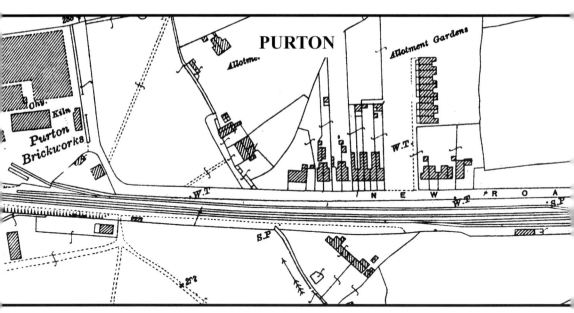

PURTON

V.   The 1923 edition includes a down refuge siding on the right. It was in use in 1901-63. On the left is the up refuge siding (1901-65) from which diverged a siding to Hill's brickworks from 1910 to 1964.

14.   The station opened with the line and thus the village had a train service before the small country town of Swindon. This eastward view from March 1958 features the wooden up building shortly before its replacement. There was a staff of seven in the 1930s. (H.C.Casserley)

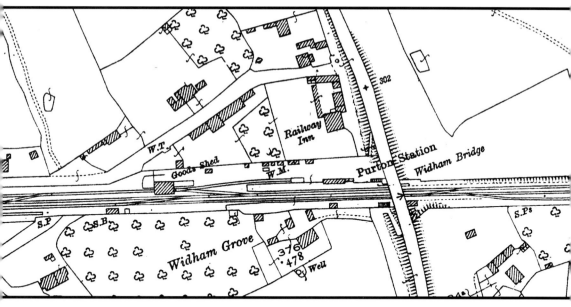

15.   Two photos from about 1960 feature the new building. This one includes the brickworks and the 37-lever signal box which lasted until 16th August 1965. Goods traffic ceased on 1st July 1963. (J.Moss/R.S.Carpenter)

16.   Passengers had little time to enjoy the new premises as service was withdrawn on 2nd November 1964. The crossover remained in use until 1965. The building was still standing in 2004 and the yard had found a commercial use. (J.Moss/R.S.Carpenter)

17.   The intricate ironwork of the stairway is clearer in this view, as is the down refuge siding. One unusual item made in the village was wax used in the production of dentures. Its population rose from 2565 in 1901 to 3295 in 1961. (Lens of Sutton coll.)

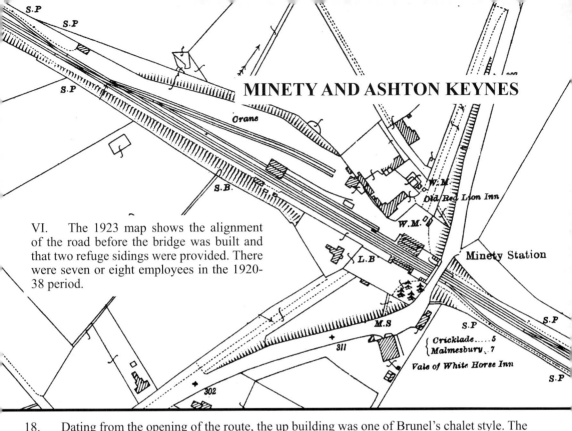

MINETY AND ASHTON KEYNES

VI.   The 1923 map shows the alignment of the road before the bridge was built and that two refuge sidings were provided. There were seven or eight employees in the 1920-38 period.

18.   Dating from the opening of the route, the up building was one of Brunel's chalet style. The footbridge was a late addition. The inn was on the route of the old road. This and the next view are from 15th March 1958. (H.C.Casserley)

19.   No. D600 speeds past the cattle dock on its way to London. The inset door on the leading coach indicates that it was one of a small batch often used on the Plymouth boat trains. (H.C.Casserley)

20.   The signal box had 31 levers and was in use from 1905 until 1968. The up refuge siding was a loop from 1943 until 1963, when this photo was taken. Note the modest goods shed when compared with others on the route. Closure dates are as for Purton. (P.J.Garland/R.S.Carpenter)

OAKSEY HALT

21.   The halt opened on 18th February 1929 and closed on 2nd November 1964. It was half a mile east of the village and was also used for milk churn traffic. (Lens of Sutton coll.)

Minety and Ashton Keynes	1903	1913	1923	1933
Passenger tickets issued	9016	11968	12496	11281
Season tickets issued	*	*	13	53
Parcels forwarded	27224	54976	41518	16105
General goods forwarded (tons)	1628	1512	1303	517
Coal and coke received (tons)	464	184	136	264
Other minerals received (tons)	1603	2386	3127	120
General goods received (tons)	2140	2022	2342	3263
Trucks of livestock handled	225	469	282	36

(* not available.)

SOUTH OF KEMBLE

22.　　Kemble Tunnel is 415yds in length and was not necessary for engineering reasons, merely to appease a local landowner. The 15.00 Worcester Foregate Street to Swindon is approaching the beginning of the 12-mile single line section southwards on 25th August 1981. (T.Heavyside)

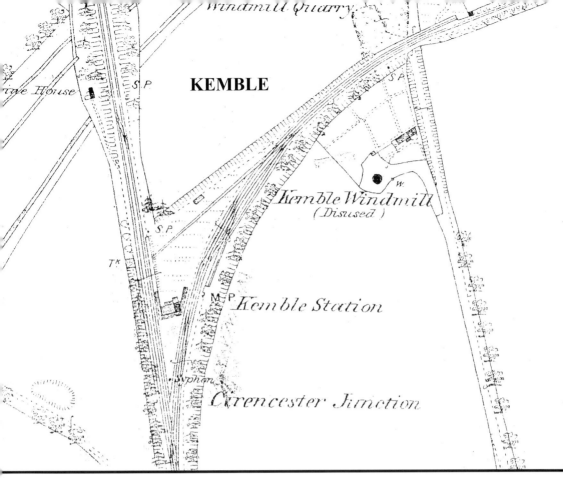

KEMBLE

Windmill Quarry.

ive House

Kemble Windmill
(Disused)

Kemble Station

Siphon

Cirencester Junction

VII.   The aforementioned landowner refused to allow the public across his land and so there was no road access to the junction until after his death. The down platform is concealed by trees on this map from about 1880. Opposite is a V-shaped platform, Cirencester trains using the right side of it.

23.   No footbridge was available at the first station, passengers using the crossing in the foreground. A minimal timber building was provided, but a generous awning was on offer. The water column has been given good protection from frost. (C.Maggs coll.)

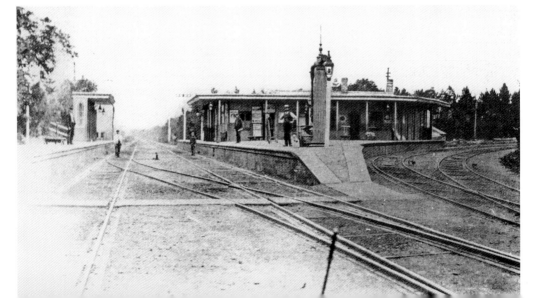

24.   The 1882 structures are seen from the road bridge, with gas tanks in the siding. On the left is East Box, which closed in 1928, along with West Box. The loco of an up train is being oiled and watered, while shunting takes place on the down line. (Lens of Sutton)

VIII.   Land was purchased in 1881 for a new station, approach roads and staff dwellings. This 1921 edition shows the result and includes the lines for the Tetbury branch on the left. The crane adjacent to the long siding was not listed in 1938.

Kemble	1903	1913	1923	1933
Passenger tickets issued	19089	21846	21643	26195
Season tickets issued	*	*	62	123
Parcels forwarded	16560	24254	18372	7027
(* not available.)				

BRITISH RLYS (W)   BRITISH RLYS (W)
288   KEMBLE   KEMBLE   288
288   TO   S.3   288
       CIRENCESTER TOWN
288   THIRD CLASS   288
       11d Z   Fare   11d Z
    Cirencester Town   CirencesterTown
     FOR CONDITIONS   FOR CONDITIONS
       SEE BACK   SEE BACK   G-L

955   2nd · SINGLE   SINGLE · 2nd   5
955   Kemble to   5
955   Kemble   Kemble   5
       Chesterton Lane Halt Chesterton Lane Halt
955   CHESTERTON LANE HALT   9
       (W)   8d. Fare 8d.   (W)
       For conditions see over For conditions see over

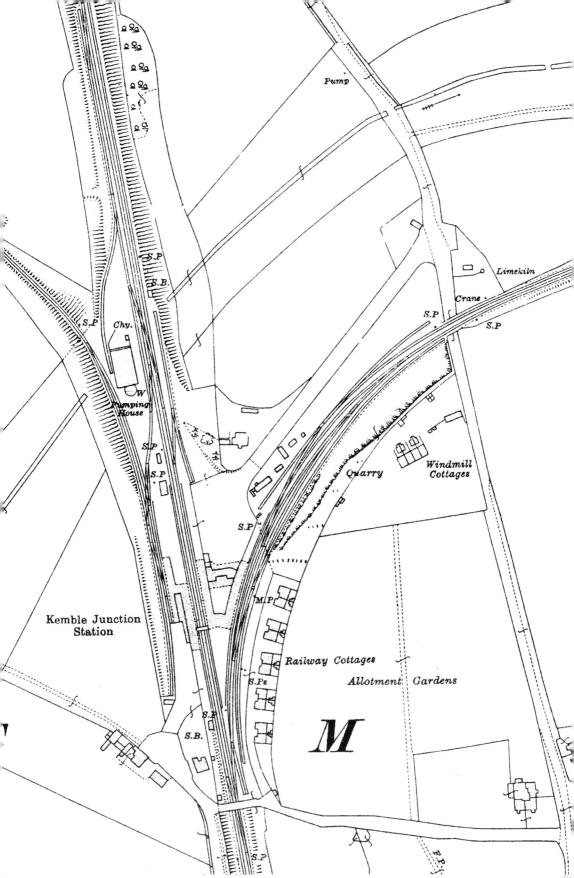

25.   We can now enjoy three peaceful photos from about 1950. Here a few bicycles are gathered around the car park sign. The station was accessible from 1st May 1882, but the terms of the land sale precluded the sale of liquor on the premises. (J.Moss/R.S.Carpenter)

26.   The Tetbury branch is on the left, behind the 1928 signal box. The supplementary high level water tank was presumably required to give adequate pressure to the railway houses. The water was originally raised by horse power; steam was used from 1872 to 1935 and electricity subsequently. (J.Moss/R.S.Carpenter)

27.　　The small yard is seen to be mainly used for permanent way materials. Most freight was conveyed to Coates (see picture 63). The stops of the long siding are in the distance. General goods traffic ceased on 19th May 1964, but coal continued until 1st August 1967. (J.Moss/R.S.Carpenter)

28.　　Mixed trains were worked on both branches. This is the 10.35am to Cirencester Town on 6th September 1952, hauled by no. 8779. The hut housed a 10-lever ground frame and the electric staff instrument for the branch. (R.M.Casserley)

29.   The same engine is seen on the same day, having returned from Cirencester. Alongside is the run-round loop, the points of which were worked from the ground frame. There had been a staff of 18 in 1929-31, probably an all-time record. (H.C.Casserley)

30.   A horsebox stands in the dock as no. 5018 *St. Mawes Castle* passes it with the 11.45am Cheltenham to Paddington on 27th April 1955. The signal box had 70 levers and was in use until 28th July 1968, when the singling to Swindon took place. (R.M.Casserley)

31.   The Tetbury branch platform was widened in 1930 so that the track could be extended to run alongside the former Co-op dock. This allowed the loop to be extended, which facilitated the handling of horsebox traffic, in particular. A mixed train is behind 0-4-2T no. 5804 in about 1956. (J.Moss/R.S.Carpenter)

32.   The Western staff did not like their brake vans wandering: R.U. means Restricted Use. Even one of the branch guards spent nearly 40 years working nowhere else. The photo is from 4th April 1964, the last day of branch operation. (J.Platt)

33.   A short length of the Cirencester line was retained by the engineers and it was often occupied by tamping machines. The picture was taken a few seconds before photo no. 22. (T.Heavyside)

34.   Kemble Tunnel is in the distance as no. 150247 approaches on 22nd March 2004, while working from Swindon to Gloucester. The station retained its dignity and siding. (M.Turvey)

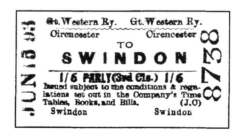

Tetbury Branch

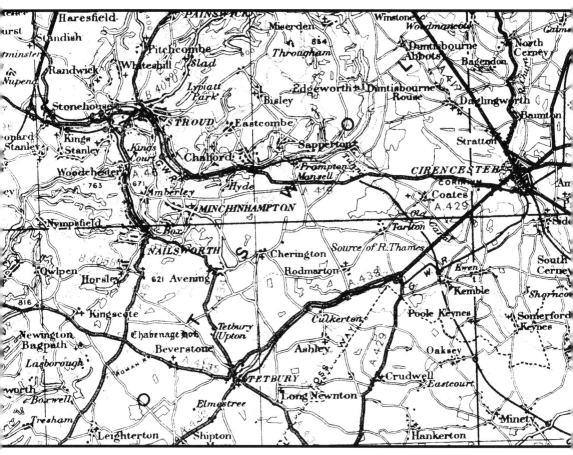

IX.   The 1946 survey is shown at 4 miles to 1 inch to include the branch, together with that to Cirencester. The north-south line through Cirencester is featured in our *Cheltenham to Andover* album.

JACKAMENTS BRIDGE HALT

35.   The shelterless structure came into use on 3rd July 1939 to convey workers constructing the nearby Kemble Airfield for the RAF. There was a through 6.50am train from Cirencester, due at 7.10, with a 5.20pm return service. After work was completed, all branch trains called here until the halt's closure on 27th September 1948. (Lens of Sutton)

RODMARTON PLATFORM

36.   The structure was on the south side of the line and it came into use on 1st September 1904. To reach this windswept location, passengers had to use an unsurfaced track; thus their numbers were few. The photo is from April 1958. (H.C.Casserley)

CHURCH'S HILL HALT

37.   This is one of the two halts opened on 2nd February 1959 with the introduction of railbuses. History was repeating itself, as the GWR had provided low level structures and folding steps on trains more than 50 years earlier. A small crowd was recorded on 28th August 1962. (T.David/C.L.Caddy)

Tetbury	1903	1913	1923	1933
Passenger tickets issued	17664	17809	14043	5895
Season tickets issued	*	*	23	2
Parcels forwarded	36038	53781	47143	16530
General goods forwarded (tons)	774	1153	957	117
Coal and coke received (tons)	827	913	703	837
Other minerals received (tons)	1723	2931	727	1784
General goods received (tons)	3040	4063	2796	815
Trucks of livestock handled	383	355	214	95

(* not available.)

Culkerton	1903	1913	1923	1933
Passenger tickets issued	3998	3740	2715	2017
Season tickets issued	*	*	27	4
Parcels forwarded	3666	4395	7334	868
General goods forwarded (tons)	429	354	396	40
Coal and coke received (tons)	-	13	132	150
Other minerals received (tons)	921	963	228	50
General goods received (tons)	405	966	979	413
Trucks of livestock handled	28	34	30	16

(* not available.)

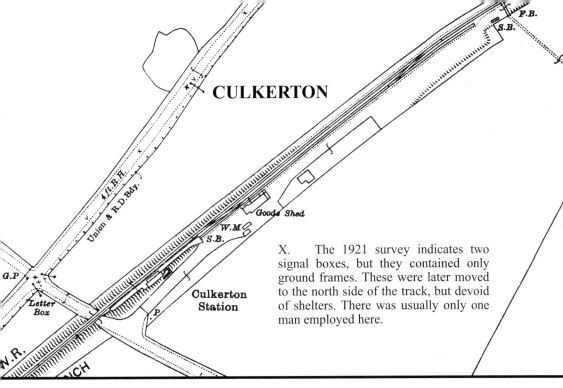

CULKERTON

X. The 1921 survey indicates two signal boxes, but they contained only ground frames. These were later moved to the north side of the track, but devoid of shelters. There was usually only one man employed here.

38. The footbridge shown on the map is in the distance, as is the loading gauge. The siding formed a loop until 1960, thus this photo is prior to that date. There was no mains water here, but eventually the goods shed was converted to a dwelling. (Lens of Sutton)

39.   Two photos from about 1950 show 2-6-2T no. 4550 with a mixed train from Tetbury. The station closed to passengers on 5th March 1956, as average figures were down to 41 per month. However, it reopened as a halt for railbuses on 2nd February 1959. (J.Moss/R.S.Carpenter)

40.   After 1956, a goods porter appeared for two hours each weekday, freight traffic ceasing on 1st July 1963. Subsequently, it was only used for goods inwards. (J.Moss/R.S.Carpenter)

TROUBLE HOUSE HALT

41.   The name was taken from a nearby 17th century inn on the A433, originally the "Waggon & Horses". A later landlord hung himself, a second drowned and in 1812 it was the centre for rioting farmworkers. The halt opened on 2nd February 1959 and was on the north side of the line. It was no trouble as there were seldom any passengers, except on the last day when a coffin full of empty alcohol bottles was despatched by an unruly crowd to Dr. Beeching in London. The train was delayed by bales of burning straw on the track. (R.M.Casserley)

2nd · SINGLE   SINGLE · 2nd
TETBURY to
Tetbury   Tetbury
Paddington   Paddington
PADDINGTON
(W)   20/9   Fare   20/9   (W
For conditions see over   For conditions see over

TETBURY

XI.   The 1921 survey shows the close proximity of the station to the town centre and the dots and dashes reveal that it was then in a different county. The boundary later moved two miles eastward.

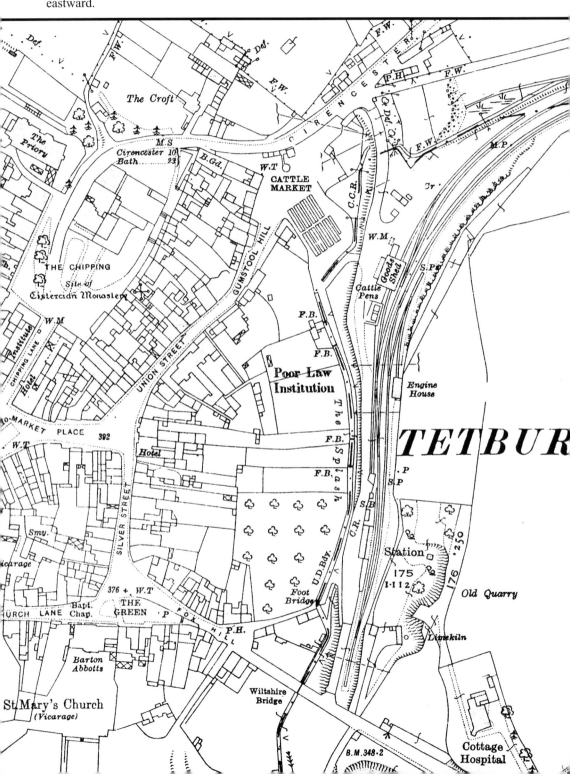

42.   An Edwardian postcard features the first building, which was of timber construction and was replaced in 1916. The locomotive appears to be a class 517 0-4-2T. There were seven or eight employees here until 1932, but mainly five thereafter. Staffing ceased on 1st September 1961. The canopy was only over the platform initially. (Lens of Sutton)

43.   The table under picture 37 shows that the main commodity inwards was coal, the exception being stone used for road improvement. Merchants and collieries owned their own wagons until World War II. This example is from 1897. (HMRS)

44.   Two photographs from 21st May 1953 show opposite ends of the platform. Two horse boxes and surplus fodder are seen near the end of the line. (Nelson coll./T.Walsh)

45.   The water tank is on the south end of the engine shed and the change of brickwork indicates the extent of its height increase since picture 42 was taken. (Nelson coll./T.Walsh)

46. The branch engine was kept here and an overnight shedman prepared it ready for the fireman who then put all things in order for the driver. This and the next two photos are from 27th April 1955. (R.M.Casserley)

47. This and the previous picture include the end loading dock, sometimes used for farm machinery. The lamp room and general store is also evident. The end of the line is in view, as is the rodding tunnel which confirms the position of the signal box, which closed in 1926. It had eight levers, plus three spare. (H.C.Casserley)

48.   No. 7418 has arrived with the 10.30am from Kemble and is about to use the spring points to run round. The point rod seen in picture 42 was removed in 1926. Such 0-6-0PTs were common in the final years, but 0-4-2Ts had been the norm previously. (R.M.Casserley)

49.   Freight service ceased on 3rd August 1963, but the yard continued to be used for coal, as seen in two photos from April 1964. The goods shed doors were replacements following a shunting accident. Adjoining the shed is the goods office and next to that is the weighbridge office. The cattle pens are on the left; it was only a short walk to the cattle market - see map. (J.Platt)

50.	The yard crane was of 6-ton capacity, whilst the one in the shed could lift 30cwt. The locomotive shed housed the branch railbus until December 1963. The shed was still standing in 2004 and the yard was in use as a car park. (J.Platt)

51.	Electric train staff operation was introduced in 1910, but a simple wooden staff was used later, probably from 1926, to the end. One room was used as a crew restroom, after 1961. The railbus was built by AC Cars who also produced luxury sports saloon cars, although not in the class of the nearby Rolls Royce. The leaking gas lights had given way to portable pressurised oil lamps used until the last day of operation, 4th April 1964. (Millbrook House)

Cirencester Branch

PARK LEAZE HALT

52.   This halt opened on 4th January 1960, almost a year after the introduction of railbuses. It was situated over one mile northeast of Ewen, on a lane to a farm, and west of the line. (Lens of Sutton coll.)

CHESTERTON LANE HALT

53.   A busy dual carriageway now passes over the site of this bridge. This view towards Kemble details the structure which opened on 2nd February 1959. It was less than half a mile from Cirencester Watermoor station. (R.S.Carpenter)

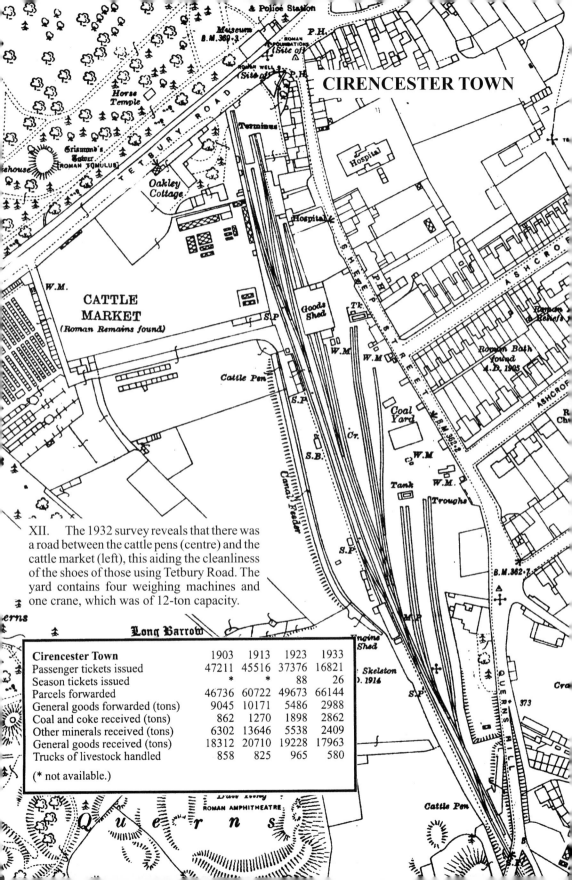

CIRENCESTER TOWN

XII.   The 1932 survey reveals that there was a road between the cattle pens (centre) and the cattle market (left), this aiding the cleanliness of the shoes of those using Tetbury Road. The yard contains four weighing machines and one crane, which was of 12-ton capacity.

Cirencester Town	1903	1913	1923	1933
Passenger tickets issued	47211	45516	37376	16821
Season tickets issued	*	*	88	26
Parcels forwarded	46736	60722	49673	66144
General goods forwarded (tons)	9045	10171	5486	2988
Coal and coke received (tons)	862	1270	1898	2862
Other minerals received (tons)	6302	13646	5538	2409
General goods received (tons)	18312	20710	19228	17963
Trucks of livestock handled	858	825	965	580

(* not available.)

54.　　Once the terminus of trains from London, only the quoins of the canopy remained in 1952. There had been an overall roof until 1874. There was a staff of 24 to 28 in the 1930s, but the photo is from the 1950s. (J.Moss/R.S.Carpenter)

55.　　Before the official suffix "Town" was introduced on 1st July 1924, the term "Sheep Street" was often used; this was east of the station. The 10.35am mixed tain from Kemble has just arrived on 6th September 1952, the main building being in the background. (R.M.Casserley)

56.　　The approach to the station is known as the throat and it is seen on a misty day in 1952, with the engine shed on the left. The dock on the right was termed "Pig Wharf" and was added in 1914, along with the four sidings on the west of the yard. (R.M.Casserley)

57.   The run-round loop is to the right of 2-6-2T no. 4542 in this view from about 1957. The sidings on the right ran to the loading docks. (R.M.Casserley)

58.   This engine shed dated from 1872 when the broad gauge one was demolished. It housed the railbus after the end of steam and is seen in August 1960. The sidings on the left served the coal yard. (R.S.Carpenter)

59.   The frontage was modernised in 1956 and is seen in May 1962, in need of a wash. An AC railbus adds another touch of modernity, as agricultural equipment is being loaded onto flat wagons. The number of tickets issued jumped from 19,262 in 1958 to 30,427 in 1959, but the boom was short lived. (Nelson coll./T.Walsh)

60.   The cattle market was held on the first and third Mondays of each month and special trains of up to 25 wagons were run, whilst the branch train would often have an extra coach. Milk was once important: 17,426 churns were despatched in 1928, but much of this traffic was lost to road transport soon after. (Nelson coll./T.Walsh)

61.   The box had only 19 levers and was in use from about 1893 until 14th June 1964. It controlled the final mixed trains in 1958; they were the 10.25am ex-Kemble and the 7.45pm from Cirencester. Electric tokens were introduced on the branch in 1945. (J.Platt)

62.   The original wooden goods shed was replaced with this steel framed structure in 1938. In the 1940s, the main goods trains were the 7.10am from Kemble and the 4.0pm return. Vast amounts of bagged fertiliser and animal feedstuff were handled. (J.M.Tolson/F.Hornby)

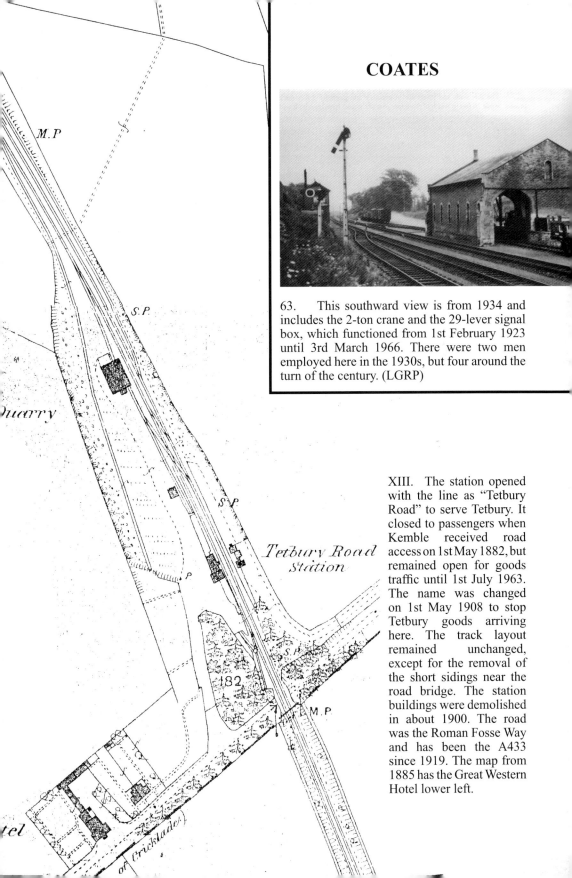

COATES

63.   This southward view is from 1934 and includes the 2-ton crane and the 29-lever signal box, which functioned from 1st February 1923 until 3rd March 1966. There were two men employed here in the 1930s, but four around the turn of the century. (LGRP)

M.P.

S.P.

Quarry

S.P.

Tetbury Road Station

P.

S.P.

182

M.P.

tel

of Cricklade

XIII.   The station opened with the line as "Tetbury Road" to serve Tetbury. It closed to passengers when Kemble received road access on 1st May 1882, but remained open for goods traffic until 1st July 1963. The name was changed on 1st May 1908 to stop Tetbury goods arriving here. The track layout remained unchanged, except for the removal of the short sidings near the road bridge. The station buildings were demolished in about 1900. The road was the Roman Fosse Way and has been the A433 since 1919. The map from 1885 has the Great Western Hotel lower left.

EAST OF CHALFORD

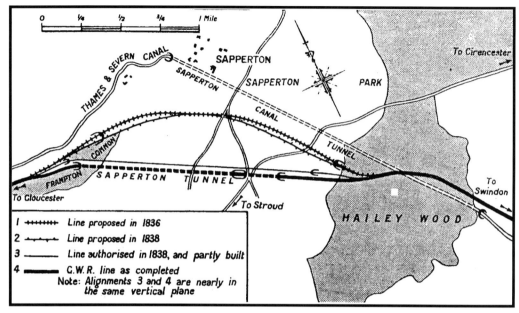

XIV.   The first tunnel was to have been 2830yds long on a gradient of 1 in 352. Brunel's second design was cheaper and slightly shorter, but steeper at 1 in 350. Much digging was undertaken on yet a further revised route, but the takeover by the GWR resulted in plan 4, which gave two shorter tunnels. Much of the climb from the west was at 1 in 60, instead of 1 in 330 of the earlier schemes. (Railway Magazine)

XV.   The section shows the final two designs and their relative inclinations. The running tunnels are 1855 and 352yds in length; the 1789 canal tunnel was over two miles long and closed in 1911, while in GWR ownership. (Railway Magazine)

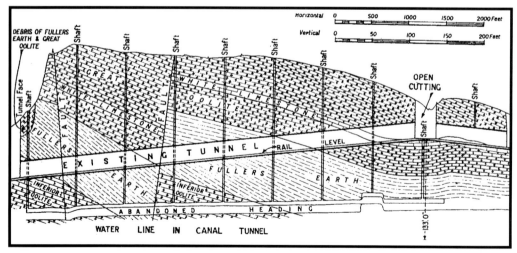

64.   No. 2920 *Saint David* struggles up the incline on the western approach to Sapperton Tunnel, with a special from Birmingham to Swindon Works on 15th June 1952. The 27-lever Sapperton Sidings signal box was east of the tunnels and in use from 1901 to 1970. Loops were available here for much of this period. (Millbrook House)

65.   Frampton Viaduct is 129yds long and ¾ mile west of the tunnel portal. This northward view of the upper end of the Golden Valley is from 28th November 1981. The nearby village is Frampton Mansell. (P.G.Barnes)

CHALFORD

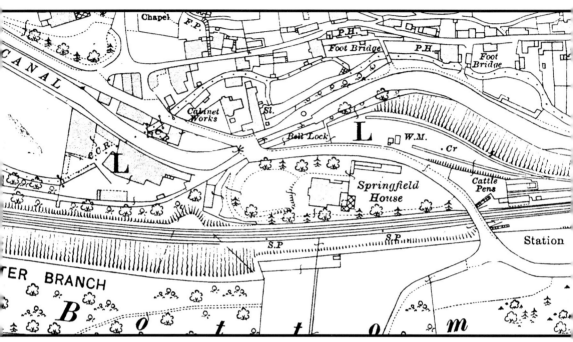

XVI. The 1922 survey has the 220yd-long Chalford Viaduct on the right and the Thames & Severn Canal above the railway on both pages.

66.   Beyond the four coaches of an up train is an autocoach and the canal is visible beyond that. The population was almost 3000 in 1901 and 2500 in 1961. The station did not open until 2nd August 1897 and much earthwork was necessary to create the goods yard. (Lens of Sutton)

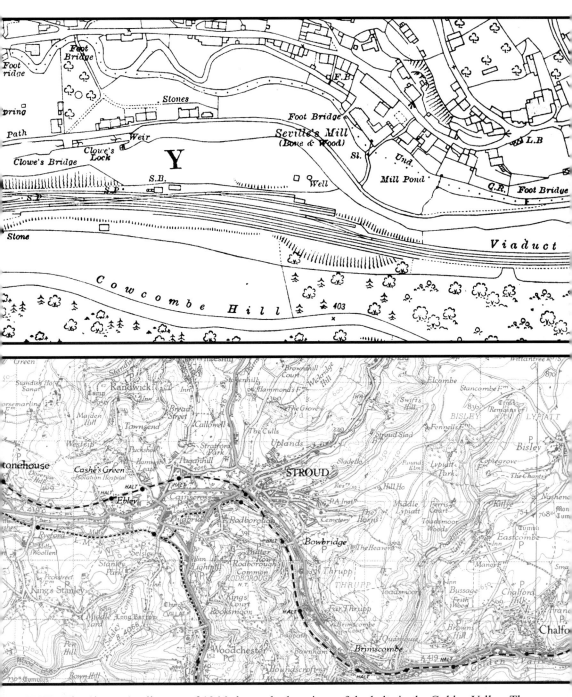

XVII. The 1ins to 1 mile map of 1946 shows the locations of the halts in the Golden Valley. The LMS branch is lower left.

67.   An eastward view from the road bridge shows the depth of the beautiful Golden Valley and the starting signal off, for two autocoaches to depart for Kemble. There was a staff of 10 here in the 1920s. (Lens of Sutton)

68.   Most autotrain workings terminated here and laid over as seen in this photo from around 1960. Both flights of steps to the road are evident. There was a level access near the two boys. There had been a loading dock on the site of the extension. (Lens of Sutton)

69.   A 2-8-0 is working a ballast train on the down line on 21st August 1960. The wagons on the left are on the site of a shed provided for a railmotor in 1903. There had been another siding to the left of it. (R.S.Carpenter)

70.   No. 6437 has reached the end of its journey with the 11.20am from Gloucester Central on 9th August 1960. There were eleven such trips on weekdays and four on Sundays at that period. The cattle dock and 6-ton crane are visible, together with the lamp room.
(D.Johnson/Millbrook House)

Chalford	1903	1913	1923	1933
Passenger tickets issued	61615	68644	81765	98109
Season tickets issued	*	*	497	282
Parcels forwarded	4516	8400	10518	7632
General goods forwarded (tons)	578	728	444	66
Coal and coke received (tons)	243	-	44	99
Other minerals received (tons)	776	573	268	321
General goods received (tons)	1860	2667	1783	305
Trucks of livestock handled	83	104	109	143
(* not available.)				

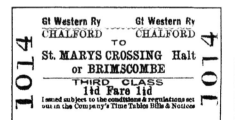

Gt Western Ry   Gt Western Ry
CHALFORD   CHALFORD
TO
St. MARYS CROSSING   Halt
or BRIMSCOMBE
THIRD   CLASS
1¼d Fare 1¼d
Issued subject to the conditions & regulations set
out in the Company's Time Tables Bills & Notices

1014   1014

2nd · SINGLE   SINGLE · 2nd

CHALFORD to
Chalford   Chalford
Stonehouse Bur t Rd   Stonehouse Bur't Rd
STONEHOUSE (Burdett Road)

(W)   1/2   FARE   1/2   (W)
For conditions see over   For conditions see over

71.   The autotrain waits to return to Gloucester not long before withdrawal of the service and station closure on 2nd November 1964. Goods traffic ceased on 12th August 1963. (M.J.Stretton coll.)

72.   No. 48650 is climbing the 1 in 75 gradient while hauling a 2-8-2T and an 0-6-0 to Swindon for scrapping. An autotrain is about to reverse on 4th April 1964. The 20 levers in the signal box were not used after 13th June 1965. (J.Platt)

ST. MARY'S CROSSING HALT

73.   This was almost one mile from Chalford and served mainly Browns Hill, which involved a climb of 300ft in altitude. The oil lamps would be attended to by the signalman. (R.S.Carpenter)

74.   The halt came into use on 12th October 1903 when the steam railmotor service to Stonehouse began. A "Castle" class 4-6-0 is tearing through with the down "Cheltenham Spa Express" on 12th June 1962. (P.J.Garland/R.S.Carpenter)

75.   In contrast, no. 8743 creeps in with an autocoach from Gloucester on the same day. The road over the crossing was unsurfaced. The crossing was still staffed more than 40 years later. Brimscombe was within sight of the signalman. (P.J.Garland/R.S.Carpenter)

Gt Western Ry CHALFORD	Gt Western Ry CHALFORD
TO	
St. MARYS CROSSING Halt	
or BRIMSCOMBE	
THIRD CLASS	
1½d Fare 1½d	

8738   8738

Issued subject to the conditions & regulations set out in the Company's Time Tables Bills & Notices

XVIII. The 1922 edition has three lines on the right. The upper one is a long refuge siding, which does not join the others on the page. It was removed in 1963; access had been from the up main line with a ground frame. It held 54 wagons.

76.　　A 1960 eastward panorama features Brimscombe East box, which had 25 levers and was functional from 1898 to 5th October 1970. It ceased to be termed "East" when the other box closed in 1964. The staff level was around 20 in the 1920s. (R.M.Casserley)

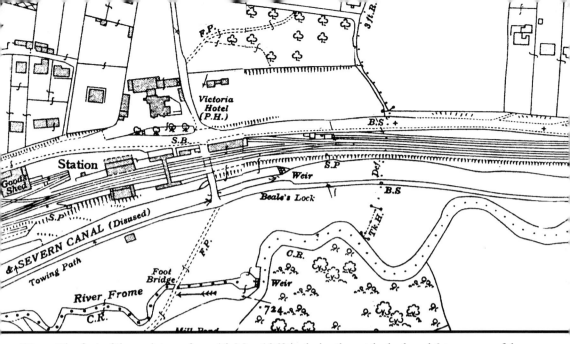

77.　The first of three pictures from 4th May 1962 includes the cattle dock and 6-ton crane of the goods yard, which closed on 12th August 1963. In the distance is West Box, which had a 17-lever frame and was only open during periods of shunting. It closed on 17th May 1964. (Nelson coll./T. Walsh)

78.   A down empty coal train stands beside the disused canal in which a weir has been built in place of a lock. On the left is the shed provided for the banking engines used to assist up trains through Sapperton Tunnel.
(Nelson coll./T.Walsh)

Brimscombe	1903	1913	1923	1933
Passenger tickets issued	22849	236707	236474	54487
Season tickets issued	*	*	494	436
Parcels forwarded	1963	8582	8568	18636
General goods forwarded (tons)	2470	3970	3364	473
Coal and coke received (tons)	331	499	262	189
Other minerals received (tons)	367	1037	594	223
General goods received (tons)	3105	4156	3863	979
Trucks of livestock handled	14	14	25	2

(* not available.)

79.   The banking engine that day was 2-6-2T no. 4163. With the advent of dieselisation, such assistance was no longer required and the shed was closed on 28th October 1963. However, locomotives came from Gloucester for a few more months, as necessary. (Nelson coll./T.Walsh)

80.   Brunel's chalet style buildings are evident in this June 1962 eastward view in which an autotrain approaches. Trains ceased to call after 2nd November 1964. (E.Wilmshurst)

BRIMSCOMBE BRIDGE HALT

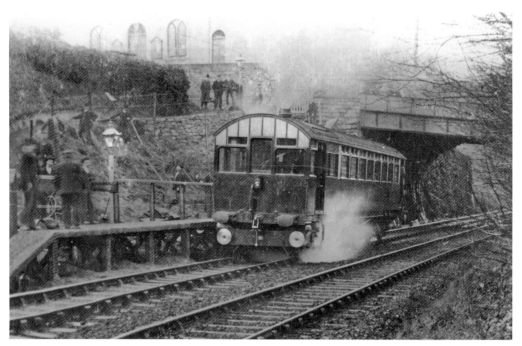

81.   Spectators are out to view the railmotor, probably on 1st February 1904, the opening day of the halt. Some labourers are still at work. (Lens of Sutton)

82.   This is the up platform, which was west of the road bridge. Both platforms closed on 2nd November 1964, some DMUs having called in the last months. (Lens of Sutton coll.)

HAM MILL HALT

83.　　The halt opened on 12th October 1903. This is steam railmotor no. 49 which is carrying a headboard showing CHALFORD AND STONEHOUSE. (Lens of Sutton coll.)

BOWBRIDGE CROSSING HALT

84.　　In less than one mile travellers came to these substantial brick platforms, which came into use on 1st May 1905. This is the view south. (W.A.Camwell/SLS)

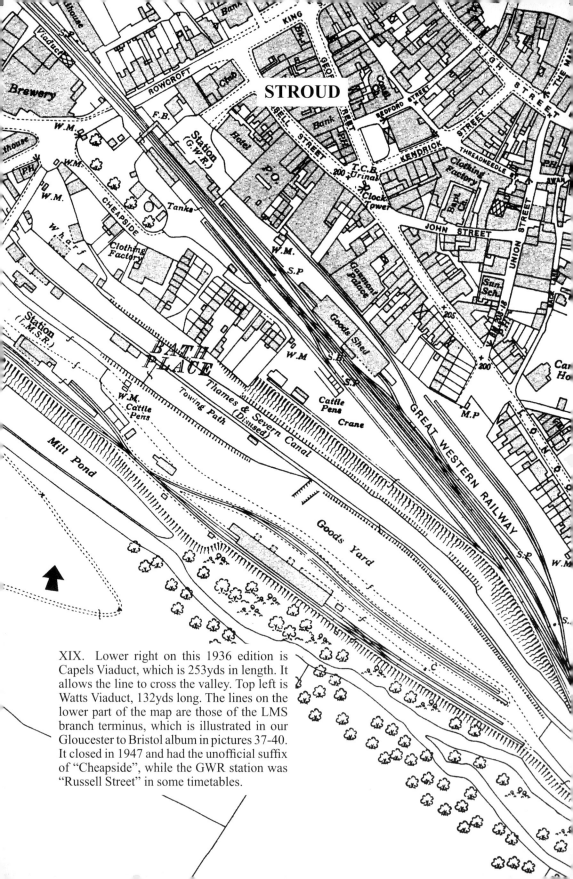

STROUD

XIX. Lower right on this 1936 edition is Capels Viaduct, which is 253yds in length. It allows the line to cross the valley. Top left is Watts Viaduct, 132yds long. The lines on the lower part of the map are those of the LMS branch terminus, which is illustrated in our Gloucester to Bristol album in pictures 37-40. It closed in 1947 and had the unofficial suffix of "Cheapside", while the GWR station was "Russell Street" in some timetables.

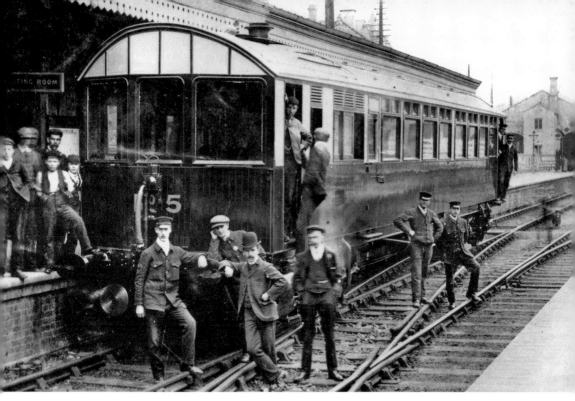

85.　Railmotor no. 5 was completed in April 1904 and it ran until May 1915. During this period the station staff level was about 30, but it rose from 63 to 75 during the 1930s. (Lens of Sutton coll.)

86.　The north elevation was recorded in about 1960, by which time the population had reached about 18,000 having risen from under 8000 in 1900. (Lens of Sutton coll.)

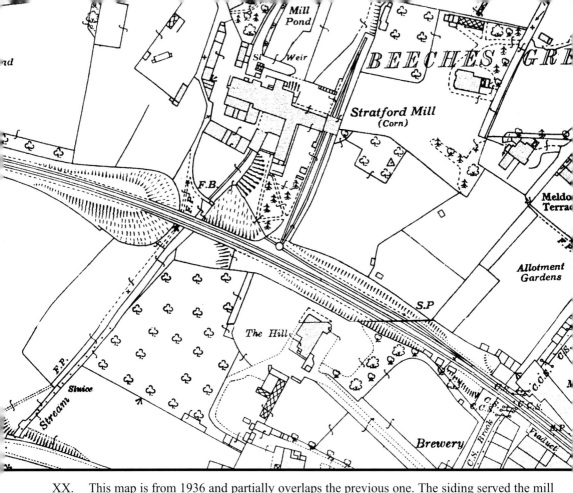

XX.   This map is from 1936 and partially overlaps the previous one. The siding served the mill of R.Townsend & Co. Ltd from 1901 to 1970.

87.   The yard crane on the right had a capacity of six tons and the signal box had 41 levers, which were in use until 5th October 1970. "Castle" class 4-6-0 no. 7000 *Viscount Portal* is passing the well buttressed goods shed. (A.W.V.Mace/Milepost 92½)

88.	The 1.3pm from Gloucester Central was worked by 0-4-2T no. 1472 on 17th July 1962. Parcels, perambulators and pigeon baskets were all part of a porter's day in that bygone era. He also had to release the pigeons. (J.Coltas/M.J.Stretton)

89.	Two pictures from May 1962 include the up bay and the railings alongside the down dock line. The GWR had once operated a bus service to Painswick and Cheltenham from this station. (Nelson coll./T.Walsh)

90.   The advent of the railmotor service in 1903 necessitated an additional water tank and increase in the size of the down platform, left. New buildings were provided on it at that time. (Nelson coll./T.Walsh)

91.   The 16.22 Paddington to Cheltenham arrives behind no. 47066 on 25th August 1981. The down yard was completely overgrown, freight service having been withdrawn on 10th July 1967. The goods shed was a listed structure and three sidings were still in place near it in 2004. (T.Heavyside)

92.   All structures were complete when Sprinter no. 150247 was photographed at the up platform on 22nd March 2004. Here is a rare example of a tree growing on a platform. The historic specimen is an American beech. (M.Turvey)

WEST OF STROUD

93.   The 17.57 Worcester Shrub Hill to Swindon DMU approaches the platform over Watts Viaduct on 25th August 1981. The structure was named after the nearby brewery. (T.Heavyside)

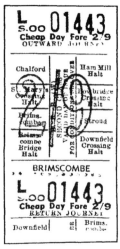

DOWNFIELD CROSSING HALT

94.   The halt opened on 12th October 1903 with the railmotor service, but the huts did not arrive until about 1920. We are less than one mile from Stroud. (Lens of Sutton)

95.   The 2.0pm service from Chalford to Gloucester was worked by ex-GWR railcar no. W19W on 9th July 1959. The route was steeply graded for these under-powered cars. (H.C.Casserley)

96.   No. 7006 *Lydford Castle* was recorded with an up express on 6th April 1963, while an old-style hurricane oil lamp hangs near the seat. The guard was responsible for the lamps at most unstaffed platforms. (G.Adams/M.J.Stretton coll.)

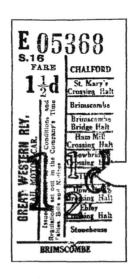

CASHES GREEN HALT

97.   This was a late addition to the list of halts, not opening until 22nd January 1930, and only half a mile from Downfield Crossing Halt. This is a westward view. (Lens of Sutton coll.)

98.   Looking east on 24th April 1958, some of the houses that justified its presence are evident. The road ran north to Randwick. (R.M.Casserley)

EBLEY CROSSING HALT

99.   The next stop was within half a mile and this opened with the railmotor service. This unit has its cylinder covers brightly burnished, probably on opening day. (Lens of Sutton)

100.   The full modernisation treatment followed: concrete platforms, rectangular huts, enamelled signs and electric lights. Cashes Green Halt is in the distance. (W.A.Camwell/SLS)

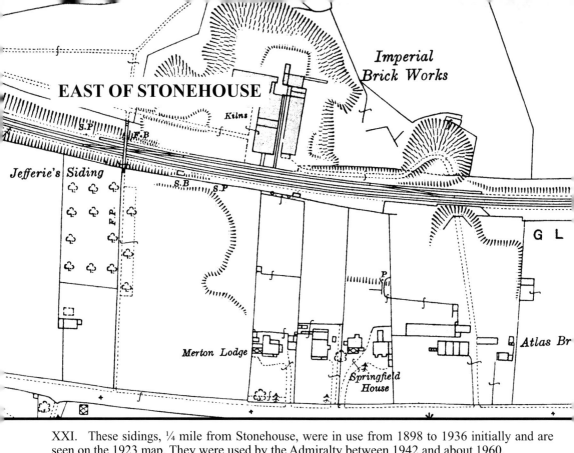

XXI. These sidings, ¼ mile from Stonehouse, were in use from 1898 to 1936 initially and are seen on the 1923 map. They were used by the Admiralty between 1942 and about 1960.

STONEHOUSE

XXII. The loop near the brickworks was its private siding, which was in use from 1891 to 1959. Each side of this 1923 map is the start of a refuge siding, which were in use in 1901-65.

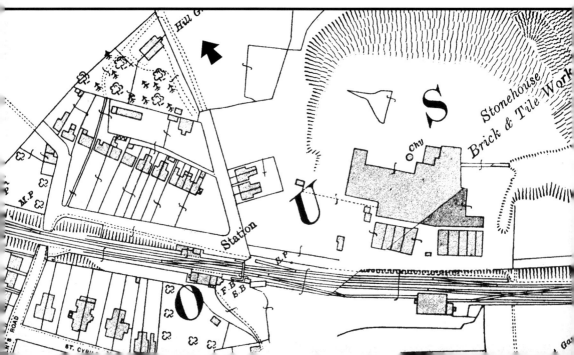

101. The chalet design is evident again in this postcard view of the up platform. The number of employees peaked at about eleven in 1913. There was a coal concentration depot in the goods yard in the 1960s. (Lens of Sutton)

102. Three photos from June 1962 give a complete survey of the historic premises. No. 1424 is at the head of the 1.15pm to Chalford on the 2nd. The crossover gave access to the brickworks from the down line. (E.Wilmshurst)

103.   Pannier tank no. 8743 is running in from Chalford on the 12th, with two vans attached. The 40-lever signal box closed on 5th October 1970. The suffix "Burdett Road" was used from 17th September 1951 until 6th May 1968, when the station on the Bristol line closed. (P.J.Garland/R.S.Carpenter)

104.   The 3½-ton crane is evident in the goods yard, which closed on 28th December 1964. Total closure was planned for 1973, but the parish council offered to pay for new (level) platforms. BR agreed, but insisted on demolition of the buildings.   However, they were listed in 1975 and so BR stopped work and threatened closure again. (P.J.Garland/R.S.Carpenter)

105.   This is the outcome of the long sad saga. Only the footbridge survived and the platforms were completed in April 1977. This is the view west in 2004. (M.Turvey)

STANDISH JUNCTION

106.   No. 90448 is running parallel to the Gloucester-Bristol double track (left) and is about to cross to the down line on 2nd October 1960. This ex-WD 2-8-0 had passed to LNER stock in 1946 and it became no.63127. There were only two tracks north of the junction after 18th August 1968. (H.C.Casserley)

107.   The lines to Swindon are on the right of this view of no. 56034 *Castell Ogwr/Ogmore Castle* on 4th August 1991. Control was from Gloucester Panel. (M.Turvey)

HARESFIELD

108.   The ex-Midland Railway tracks are on the left in this northward view from 1964. There were platforms only on the Bristol route and they were in use from 1854 until 1965. (Stations UK)

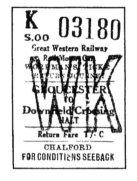

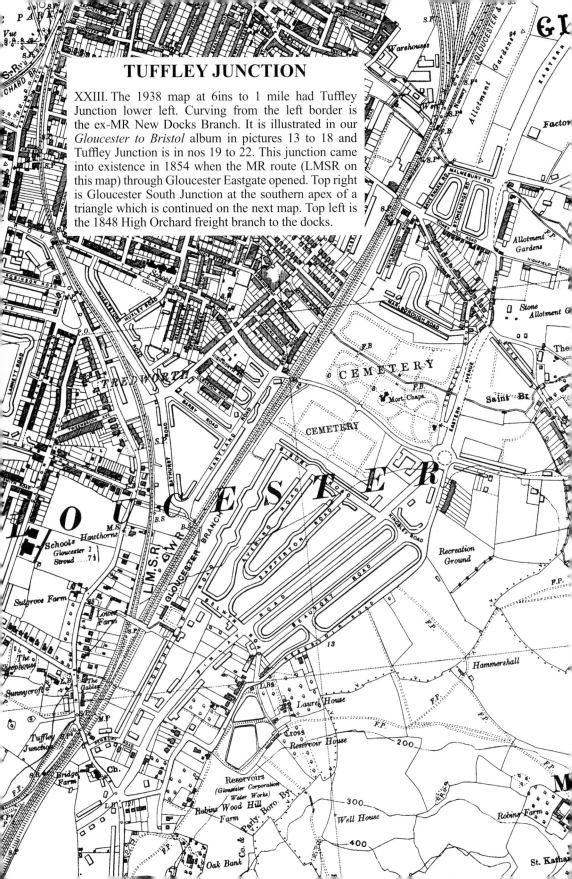

TUFFLEY JUNCTION

XXIII. The 1938 map at 6ins to 1 mile had Tuffley Junction lower left. Curving from the left border is the ex-MR New Docks Branch. It is illustrated in our *Gloucester to Bristol* album in pictures 13 to 18 and Tuffley Junction is in nos 19 to 22. This junction came into existence in 1854 when the MR route (LMSR on this map) through Gloucester Eastgate opened. Top right is Gloucester South Junction at the southern apex of a triangle which is continued on the next map. Top left is the 1848 High Orchard freight branch to the docks.

109.   The junction layout has changed several times, but this is the arrangement since 1st December 1975, when the Tuffley Loop and Eastgate station closed. The New Docks Branch had curved right in the background until its closure in 1971. SLOA's 08.25 Ealing Broadway-Hereford 13-coach charter "The Red Dragon", with preserved BR class 4 4-6-0 no. 75069, and LMS "Jubilee" class 4-6-0 no. 5690 *Leander* approach Gloucester on 28th June 1986. In the background had been Quedgeley Depot which had extensive munitions sidings during both world wars and after the last one. The RAF was responsible latterly. (S.P.Derek)

2nd-SINGLE SINGLE-2nd
Stroud to
Stroud   Stroud
Bowbridge Cr'ing Ht.   Bowbridge Cr'ing Ht.
or Downfield C. Halt   or Downfield C.Halt
BOWBRIDGE CROSSING HALT OR
DOWNFIELD CROSSING HALT
(W)   2d.   FARE   2d.   (W)
For conditions see over For conditions see over

EAST OF GLOUCESTER

110.   We can now enjoy two photos taken on 5th September 1964 at the triangle's western apex shown at the centre of the next map. It was known as Tramway Junction, as the horse-worked 1810 line of 3ft 6ins gauge between Cheltenham and Gloucester Docks crossed the tracks here in the early years. The junction was renamed Horton Road Junction in 1968. The level crossing under the third vehicle is on its site as 2-6-2T no. 4564 proceeds towards Cheltenham, the Gloucester lines diverging on the left. The signal box was in use until a panel box was opened on the left on 25th May 1968. (T.David/C.L.Caddy)

111.   This is a westward view from the other side of the track as no. 6437 departs for Chalford. The Cheltenham lines are on the left and beyond them are some of the 21 sidings of the ex-MR Barnwood Yard. In the background is the engine shed of the same name; the ex-GWR one was to the left of this view. (T.David/C.L.Caddy)

112. Here is the west end of the former GWR shed on 1st November 1959 and included is no. 7926 *Willey Hall* and 2-6-0 no. 7312. Steam traction ceased here on 10th October 1965, having begun on these premises in 1854. The allocation of 65 engines in 1947 had dropped to 35 in 1965. The code was 85B. (P.J.Kelley)

113. The three sheds on the right of the previous picture were demolished leaving the diesels to stand over the pits in the open. Nos 25211 and 25203 were recorded on 16th September 1975. (T.Heavyside)

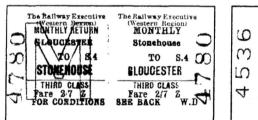

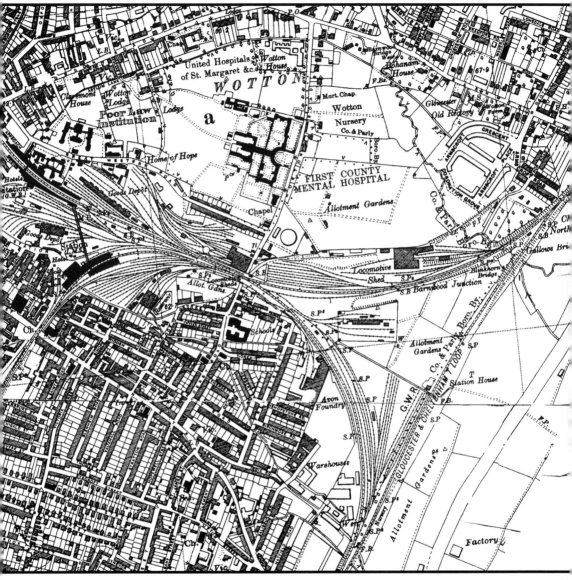

XXIV. The line to Cheltenham is on the right and the one to South Wales on the left of this continuation from the previous map. On this line is the GWR station, which was "Central" from 17th September 1951 to 26th May 1968 while the one below it was "Eastgate". The latter is extensively illustrated in Gloucester to Bristol, as it was mainly used by trains on that route. The first termini had been on the site between them. Some coaches of London-Cheltenham trains between 1847 and 1851 were detached at T Station (lower right), turned on a turntable and hauled to the GWR terminus. Note that the two main stations are connected by a long footbridge. Paddington-Cheltenham trains used Eastgate only between 1964 and its closure in 1975. Reversal has been necessary at other times. The "New Yard" sidings within the triangle were adapted for use by the engineers and, for a period from 1987, some were used for Speedlink freight traffic until its cessation in 1991. None are now in use and an elevated highway crosses the site from east to west.

114. The Royal Train stands at the down platform on 23rd June 1909, with Middle Box towering above it. The crossover allowed two trains to use the platform simultaneously. In 1923, there were 127 employed on goods work and 106 on passenger operations. (Lens of Sutton)

115. Standing under the intricate ironwork of the main entrance on 25th August 1956 is no. 1430 with an autocoach bound for Cinderford. (J.Edgington)

Other views of this station appear in *Gloucester to Bristol* and *Worcester to Hereford*, which includes the branch from Ledbury.

116.   Approaching the down platform on 10th February 1957 are "Moguls" nos 7308 and 5388. On the left is part of the long goods shed, featured on the map. On the right of the train is East Box, which was used until 1968. The signals on the right are on the line from Eastgate station. (N.W.Sprinks)

117.   The up bay was often the resting place for the Chalford autotrain, which provided such a valuable service to the Golden Valley for so long. (C.L.Caddy coll.)

118.   A transitional photo from 16th September 1975 includes part of the footbridge to Eastgate (left). The one to the up platform had vanished, as this had been used for parcels only since 1968. Temporary buildings were provided near the short canopy. No. 46044 is passing the goods shed which was still in use. (T.Heavyside)

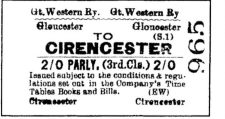

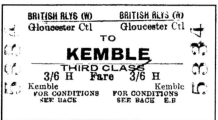

119.   New featureless buildings were officially opened on 8th March 1977 and are seen behind no. 45125 with a Cardiff to Newcastle train on 3rd November 1979. Behind the camera is platform 1, a continuation of no. 2. Its shelter is shown in the next picture. Platform 3 was the bay behind the end of the train. (T.Heavyside)

120.   The up platform (left) was restored to passenger use in 1984, necessitating a new footbridge from which this photo of an HST was taken on 23rd November 1988. Three sidings remained behind platform 4 (left) in 2004, but most of the others had been abandoned or lifted. (F.Hornby)

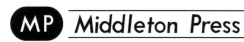
MP **Middleton Press**

Easebourne Lane, Midhurst West Sussex. GU29 9AZ

A-0 906520 B-1 873793 C-1 901706 D-1 904474

OOP Out of Print at time of printing - Please check current availability **BROCHURE AVAILABLE SHOWING NEW TITLES**
Tel:01730 813169   www.middletonpress.com   email:info@middletonpress.co.uk